The Poet's Way

Orlando C. Rowe

An Imprint of Powered to Empower Book Publishers.

The Poet's Way

Contact: contact@poweredtoempower.com

Edited By: Okorie Godsmith.

Published By: Powered to Empower Book Publishers

Dedication

For my beautiful daughter: Zarah Acacia Rowe.

I love you more than I can ever express. I hope that one day you will be inspired by these poems. This is specifically in celebration of your second birthday. May you grow as a flower unto God.

Table of Contents

Love

Faith

About This Collection

Hello, my name is Orlando Rowe, the author behind this collection of poems, **'The Poet's Way'**. I hope that as you read through, you will find the courage to be strong. My intention is to motivate you to challenge the terrains of despair with the power of faith. Your faith can make you whole. "There is no challenge too great for you to conquer," is what I found as I wrote these lines. My greatest strength has always been the power I find when I trust in God. This theme resonates throughout these poems and I implore you to Trust in God. As you read, dissect each line and hear the sound of triumph all around.

Over the years, as I struggled to stay afloat, I found a sense of expression through my poems. Each line tells the story of a man who has challenged the odds with spiritual tenacity. This is a very soulful collection, some are inspiring, some spiritual, but these poems all motivate you to be and to seek better. Delve into this ocean of rhyme and rhythm and experience the life changing impact of 'The Poet's Way'. As you read, may you be Blessed!

Motivational...

I Believe

If I tire when I'm rowing,

I shall reap what I'm sowing...

Cutting waves as I endure,

I will challenge it some more!

If I faulter when I'm trying,

I still hold to what is mine!

For in the storm the vessel ages,

Yet I gain my wages!

And it profits me a thing,

To hold to that which I cling!

I make a claim when I believe it,

Knowing that I receive it....

Dwelling daily in my resolve,

Holding firm until I evolve!

I stay assured lest I'm deceived,

For I did win when I believed!

A Dad's Great Sacrifice

He awaits the moon to go away,

To arrive and to challenge the day!

Toiling daily, to pay his family's price,

What love? "A Dad's great sacrifice!"

He armours himself with a might,

Surviving daily in his own plight...

Marching to victory, falling once, rising twice,

What love? What love? "A Dad's great sacrifice!"

Against all odds, he assembles in his position,

And he remembers his mission...

Surely, he commits, he conquers the device,

His Love! His love! "A Dad's great sacrifice!"

Indeed, our dads are special too,

Without our dads what would we do?

He stands at the foundation, he will suffice,

We are held together by a "Dad's great sacrifice".

And his words disarm our fears,

Things he'll do to show he cares...

He is for sure, the very form of Christ,

What Love? His Love! "A Dad's great sacrifice!"

Singular

In a singular world, I'm a singular being,
At a singular time, I'm a singular stream!
I'm a singular beam, that shines the earth,
I'm the product of the dust, son of the dirt!

Yet in a singular sphere, I have a singular hope,
That Jah is ever by me as I cope!
In a singular pain, is a singular space,
I cling to a one and singular grace!

I have a singular cry, with a singular creed,
A singular heart, with a singular need!
Yet on a singular way, Christ walks with me,
On a singular line, He talks with me!

I'm a singular man, I'm a singular son,
A singular plan, on a singular run!
Oh, who is me? I am undone,
I'm a singular strain under the sun!

In a singular world, I'm a singular beam,
At a singular time, I'm a singular stream!

Till I Dawn

I press till I dawn,

Till the morning comes home!

Until there's arrival,

Till then will I roam!

I press till I hurt,

Till I embrace what I'm worth.

I'm weak, still I rise,

Till I'm poised at the prize!

I will reach till it ends,

Until my glory descends!

And I conquer the sin,

Till I pamper the win!

When the fight is intense,

I brace my defense!

Oh, my reign will go on,

Still I pain, till I dawn!

In Thy arms I will hide,

In Your love I abide!

I soar to endure with a might,

And insists to persist till the light!

Hidden

Highly overridden, in clefts concealed,

A brave bold soul yet cornered beneath!

In crying chains, as a repentant yield,

Stunted in furrows, an incessant bleat!

Oh, the fortified walls of fear are steep,

The dungeons of despair are deep...

For they encamp a light's outburst,

The wells of God could quench such thirst!

A hidden lion shall search for Zion,

A crying bold seeks a shoulder to cry on!

Oh, the treasure of a heart's detained,

Yet the bells of freedom are unchained!

These bells shall sing a song,

The sound of triumph shall ever prolong...

So hidden, a peculiar piece as I,

Yet the wells of Jah shall pamper by!

Sometimes

Sometimes we rise, other times we fall,

Even when we are quiet, at times we call.

Sometimes there is horror as we go,

The whilst of life we do not know.

And many times, we bawl, we bawl,

When we cannot run, sometimes we crawl...

Yet we challenge our griefs in the middle of the night,

In the crevices of the plight, in the battle we must fight!

There are times when life's stench is at hand,

When we orbit our mountains in a distant land.

Yet these are times, times when we say,

For sure, for sure, there is a brighter day!

Trod on, trod on, you in despair,

You must go on and on I dare!

Fight your fear, as fierce as the sun,

On and on till time is done!

Oh, you who hurt, oh you who bleed,

Oh, you who travel with a heavy creed...

It's with us all, for sometimes we fall,

Yet even when we are quiet, God hears our bawl!

Heavy Heart

Heavy Heart, Light Tears,

Piercing fears through the years.

Yet God He knows and cares,

With me, my burden bears.

Plump pains, through bitter veins,

Lasting stains on fortified chains.

Still; redemption songs remain,

Songs of praise drill my brain.

As birth pangs prick, the slit of thorns,

I'm weathered daily, whipped and worn.

Bricked and burred in a solitary space,

But the strings of Jah, they bid me grace.

How I look upon His face, incarcerated,

As I walk this lane, I'm heavily weighted.

My cries remain, filled with crave,

For the fingers of God to come and save.

Heavy heart, light tears,

Piercing fears, through the years!

Breath of Hope

I sigh with great size,

Rainy days in my eyes.

Yet I rise, on par with the prize,

A breath, my hope supplies!

And I sigh, my agonies pamper by,

I try, though pains multiply!

When the chain of yesterday is nigh,

This breath of hope lifts me high!

And I try, I'll press till I die,

Till I awake the fire, I brace the brier!

The wells shall catch the rain I cry,

As I row my boat, I defeat my dire!

And I sigh, my heart's clock clicks of hope,

I tire from a distance spiral way…

I trod into tomorrow, up the steepest slope,

Yet this breath of hope brightens my day!

A Fight

It's a fight, up a hill, with a might,

It's a drill, to a height, what a plight?

Still a fight, still a strain, as a dew from a rain,

What remains is a pain, a heart with a chain!

So lost, so torn, hands so worn, eyes so blurred,

Crooked is the way, stacks of thorns, packed and burred.

Still, a wind with a whirl fills my soul with the world,

A world where cries are heard, where Alpha is the Word!

The Alpha and Omega, beginning and the end is a friend,

Indeed, every song is a hope for a garment's rend…

For a grope with a groan, is a crown from a stone,

This stone cannot be moved; a rejected stone stands alone!

On the Rock is the Crown, no death cannot hold me down,

I'm never bound amidst the rails, resurrection prevails...

Every sound is a hail, hail Him King of Kings,

My heart it claps, my soul it sings, hail Him King of
Kings!

Do You

Do you hear the mar on my breath?

You see the scar of my hands!

As raindrops drip in a pile of sacred sweat,

I'm flooded on the grounds where I stand!

Do you feel my painful little ray?

The tears from my lips when I pray!

Or the bile of my heart is it known?

There is a song from the place that I've grown…

A sad tearful song that bawls for grace,

Do you see the remnant that stains my face!

I stand in my place; I shall sing till I'm heard,

The bells of my heart shall reach my Shepherd!

Do you see these rhythms I rhyme?

My poverty of mine, the depravity I chime!

See me I plea, see the drip that I sweat,

Hear the music of the mar of my breath!!!

Real Wounds

These are real wounds; they belittle me,
Wounds beyond which I cannot see.
They cut so deep and mar so long,
These are wounds that break the strong…

Real wounds, wounds that put you in a cell,
These are wounds that scar so well.
They pierce so deep and slice so broad,
These wounds they leave a lot of flawed.

Oh, wounds of mine, real wounds of mine,
Wounds that leave me ever crying.
Wounds of mine, yet Jah shall hear,
He helps me up in my despair.

He heals the wounded one,
He strengthens the broken through His Son.
And In real wounds, as in wounds of mine,
My Christ, He rescues every time!

The Young Man's Cry

They don't see the tears the young man cries,
They don't see the times when the young man tries…
The young man's sigh, they don't hear his song,
But they do see the wrongs when the young man's wrong…

The need he harbors in greed they ignore,
They don't know the times when he is not sure…
They don't feel his pain, they don't see his trials,
but they do see the filth in the young man's files…

I hear the resounds of the young man's way,
I see him as he steps into everyday…
His broken soul, his wounded will,
I see in the distant the young man's ill…

The young man's hill, so steep and steady,
There is great need to get the young man ready…
They don't see the cries in the young man's eyes,
The young man sighs, he looks to the prize…

Yet I see the young man on his way,
I walk with him proudly every day!

I'm Lost

I'm lost, I'm not fine,

For time cannot rewind…

The place I go, I just don't know,

And so, I'm lost on this death row!

Oh, I'm away from what is real,

I cannot feel the things I feel…

I cannot heal from this distress,

My pillow so drenched in loneliness!

I'm a blunted broken bone,

I'm the story of what was sown…

And I cannot see, I have no sight,

In the flight's great height, I fight!

Still, I'm a warrior to be realized,

I chant a song with rainy eyes….

Though lost, not fine, and paths are fade,

I press to the land my Master made!!

A promised land I relentlessly hound,

In a land of promise, the lost is found….

I'm not bound, though rails encamp around me,

I chant a Psalm, 'Ahh, yes, I'm free; with Jah, I'm free!!'

In the Dark

In the darkness of the dark,

Often souls find spark.

In the grave, in solitude,

Something cradles in the brood!

And often depths derail,

Sightlessness can hinder sail.

Yet dark awakes a light,

It's what happens after night…

For life is roused a deep,

Our flames find franchise as we sleep!

And lest a seed be gone away,

A seed is not rescued in the day!

Still, faith finds courage when it's tested,

Death finds power resurrected…

Nothing can't hold me down,

If I die, I must rebound!

And at the darkest side of dark,

In Christ, my soul shall spark!

For I find cradle in the deep…

And in my spirit, I'll ever leap!!

Dreams

The dreams I dreamed, they scream,

At me, in me, with me, crying; redeem!

For I've slept, as darkness intercepts me,

But the dreams I dreamed shall set me free!

Visions in the night, clasping tight,

As I plight, I might endure if I fight.

Visions in the night, they haunt my place,

They unravel my space and revamp my case!

I mustn't rest till I reach, till I reach,

Dreams I dreamed incessantly preach!!

And the distant truth awakes my youth,

The dreams I dreamed shall ever recruit…

Are the dreams I dreamed, redemption songs,

They awake the bells, bells that bong!

Dreams I dreamed, they guide me along,

The dreams I dreamed, **'Redemption Songs'**!!

Secret Songs

Some most sacred songs are secret songs,

Songs we sing in the plight of night.

The strings of praise, when the pang prolongs,

When the soul is anguished by an enduring fight…

Precious praises are of pricks and chains,

A melody united in strings of pains…

Most sacred songs are left unheard,

When the heart's stench stains, the vision's blurred...

Yet we anchor, for we are stronger in the brood,

For the light of the brave is bright, the dark's eschewed...

And the songs we sing at plight, are worship songs,

Songs that utter worthy, are days when the pang prolongs!!

Secret songs, when the heart's cry sighs,

A tune of glory that convinces us to rise…

Are the songs we sing at night,

Bangs of precious praise, when we endure our fight.

I Am

Like a gallop on a trail,

Against the wind, as a sail…

I'm a hope with a breath,

For a journey unto death…

I'm a shield that quenches darts,

The fuel of a failing heart…

I'm the life that cannot die,

And I'm a man who will ever try!

I'm a star that ever shines,

And I'm the lost that ever finds…

A breathless breath that breathes eternal,

I'm a benevolently vicious animal!

I'm a grain that will surely die,

A resurrection that blossoms by and by!

And I'm the trail that tracks the cross,

And I'm the sail that glides across…

A vulnerable little man, am I,

A rebel unto Jah, am I…

And though my heartaches multiply,

I'm a man who will ever try!!

Music of the Bows

I hear the sounds of the rain,

Warring against the grains...

Crippling all the chains,

Till they are slain, every vain!!

It's the music of the bows,

When they prick the dermis…

When the strike of His arrow blows,

It's a chase without a bliss!!

For there's a melody undesired,

When man and His maker meet…

And Jah he heats the heats,

In the fryer is a fire that he wired!!

The strings strain at the mold of the clay,

When the Potter with His fingers play!

But for the joy set before, the vessel must endure,

From the lure to the cure, then the pure!!

Then there's a bloom from the tomb,

When man endures his groom!

And the music of His bow blows,

Though man has died, it's that he rose!

Thankful

Today I'm thankful, for the heavenly feasts,

For the ray that pierces my soul with peace!

I'm thankful, for the joy on my platter,

That my Christ is risen, and my enemies scatter!

Oh, the gratitude, that's fierce as a roar,

For if I knock; when I knock, He opens the door...

And I'm thankful for the bounteous flow,

The scripts of His fingers and the mercies they show!

Jah knows the lines of the faults of the quakes,

He arranges the breadth and the width it takes…

And I parade in praise when His Kingdom comes,

When He plays my heart like the harps and the drums!

I'm thankful for the storms and their doctrines,

The bows and the arrows and the pricks from the pins…

For had I not been afflicted my soul would burn,

Every lesson they teach are the lessons I learn…

Oh, the benignity of His divinity, the trace of grace,

I'm thankful for the thorns of His embrace…

For if I despise His ways, I couldn't be son,

So, I'm thankful for all and ungracious for none!

Silent Cry

Oh tears, why you run from my eyes?

Why you scar on my bruises and never realize?

You rain, yet never rectify my pain,

How you shadow my merry and trespass my sane…

The memories awake you at rest,

And when lonely, I pamper you best.

Oh, droplets of hurt, you craft my grave,

You've clouded the sunshine and joy you enslave.

You attack, amidst the will to go on,

And the weakness inside breaks me at dawn…

Still, I challenge the grief I now know,

And I fight the expression I show.

You've been a friend for long,

The reason I'm not strong.

Oh tears, could you go and never be by,

Run away with the wind and never reply.

A Ray of Hope

A ray of hope abides within the heart,

Like toddlers grasping anchor and juveniles how they start.

Courage is a need, in a horrendously beautiful way,

A ray that shapes the blessing has come this gentle day.

Their hurtful little fingers play with the birth of the ground,

The music of their pain is a dreadful sad old sound.

Hear them, Mercy Giver, oh Him who gives, who takes,

Pamper when they hunger, sap just on their aches.

They conquer through their slippage, firm upon a stance,

Like a lion on a throne, as lowly as the ants.

And the sun, how it nests upon their naked faces,

Teardrops on their nostrils, a sigh of joy replaces.

These streets, those corners of bitter mouths are crowded,

Passers seeking produce, of women who mask their heads.

Their spirits show their anger, their merits convey an aim,

Survival is compulsory, from the doors out which they came.

I utter in a silence, of a painful narrative,

My wishes ever hampered, with a willing heart to give.

But prayers have such meaning, pamper them oh Jah,

That their aches and pain will non-exist, hear me good Jehovah.

Family

I'm captured by the smiles that their faces show,

How much I love them all, they just wouldn't know.

In all I do, moments I breathe, in this life that I live,

 Family is a gift only God could give!

 I'm comforted by the thought that it'll be fine,

In the presence of loved ones, I feel joy divine.

I peak in all happiness, to commune with the splendor I see,

In an atmosphere of peerless joy, they help my being to be!

I disregard the differences, to keep the light awake,

I pamper their tears through times they might ache.

Like a fish in the ocean, as a bird in the wild with a song,

When I'm a distance away, I realize there is where I belong.

I feel success through their times of achievement,

We face them together, times of bereavement.

In all I do, moments I breathe, in this life that I live,

Family is a gift only God could give!

Great Men

Oh, great men, who trod the rocky road,

Great men, who bear a burden's heavy load.

They reach to find; the mission is never done,

Oh, great men, who labour under the sun.

Strong men, who walked across the netted ends,

Strong men, who the nations they defend.

They conclude to know the mission is never complete,

Oh, strong men, who labour on their naked feet.

They reach across the dark of night,

Oh, great men who endure the fight.

Just to know their heart's all rested,

For great things through their hands manifested.

Why do great men die, why'd they go so soon?

To watch the stars at night, and rest under the moon.

They are great men, who trod the rocky road,

Great men, who bear a burden's heavy load.

The Inner Man

You gaze and stray; you look then turn away,

You judge a cover in which plenitudes of beauty stay.

The beauty of a soul lies within its inner being,

Beneath the coat of the cover, every beauty's seen.

You drift like a river; you sway with the mind,

But the charm of the heart is beneath the blind.

The imagery of the superficial, it tells a different tale,

Perception is an opinion, but the spirit shall prevail.

I go in anger of human nature till I come to know,

That God is so great, He sees you deep below.

He sees the content of passion within the palest eyes,

He pampers the source where all such beauty lies.

You gaze and stray; you look then turn away,

Why judge a cover in which all its beauty stay?

To Our Sister

Dear sister, you are a gift forever,

As family, your joy has been our one endeavor.

So, on this your special day we say,

ENJOY! ENJOY! ENJOY! Oh, happy Birthday!!

The distance has taken you a while,

But still, you resonate and conquer every mile.

Your family loves you well, though you're far away,

ENJOY! ENJOY! ENJOY! Oh, Happy Birthday!!

Let God give you affection,

As the current maintains connection.

And never cease to rise and victory to obey,

This is what the family says, Happy Birthday!!

Daddy looks from the heavenly star,

And see the beauty that you are.

And sure, He joins with us to say,

ENJOY! ENJOY! ENJOY! Oh, HAPPY Birthday!!

Back Home

I feel the pain of being back home,

I feel the rain; indeed, I roam.

The clouds in the sky are dare once more,

Deep in the night, I cannot snore!

I smell the fragrance of my past,

And once again, I'm trapped and cast.

Down in my heart, I'm so on my own,

I once again am left alone!

I taste the bile of things I fear,

I see in the distance nothing clear…

Thoughts of then, they now come new,

I cry on the tears that I once knew!

And the more that the time goes by I crave,

For rescue the same, from this my grave!

Indeed, is the pain of being back home,

I swim in the rain; in tides I roam!

Remains

The days rush like sand across the hours,

And I await a shadow to brighten up like flowers.

The weeks pass by in no delay, I wait...

At times I'm angered and pray; sometimes I lose the faith!

I disseminate my desire; my heart perspires in tears,

As a child that slips the way, I drown in my despair.

I rekindle from slumber; I restore my hope,

But the thoughts of the morrow steepen my slope...

I collaborate with friends; they face the same,

We battle together, all at one aim!

The valleys know own burdens, oceans cry our pain,

A pardon from distress, we whisper in vain…

And the more we slip the past, the plight prolong,

I totter like a drunkard, singing a sad old song!

Deep In our sights, the memory of yesterday stains,

The days rush across, and all that was 'Remains!'

I Rise

Nothing to hold its embers from a spark,

There's no force to prevent light in the dark!

For the moment there Is, I nurture the prize,

If ever I fall, ten times I Rise!

The sooth of great joy is around,

Courage that soars is abound.

And what doesn't kill will open my eyes,

Till life is no more, I shall Rise!

I found it my will to survive,

With the courage that keeps me alive.

And no falter is greater in size,

Whenever I fall, ever I Rise!

God's ever near as I grow,

He's exalted yet pampers me low,

Oh, I side with the ways of the wise,

Jah anchors my fall, and forever I RISE!

Press On

Press on broken solider, against great defeat,

Trod on wounded sister, against the odds complete!

You are great; your potential is not known,

Press to victory mama, for the victory is your own!

Rise up lowly friend; thoughts will give you rest,

You are a mighty warrior, courageous one, confess!

That's how great you are, realize oh friend, oh friend,

You are an inevitable cause, the times recommend.

Break the shackles that once brought you pain,

Fight the battles and let the victories rain!

Press on to glory; press if ever you hurt,

Glory is ever ours, press for what you're worth!

Oh friend, Oh friend, Oh friend,

Press on to the very end,

For time and chance is for us all,

For God is great, He hears our call!

The Paradox of Yesterday

In the great paradox of yesterday,

Comfortably we set to stay…

In the good, we conquer the better,

As we partake the olden letter!

Yet it's true that we should go,

To a place we do not know…

Into the land of promise, on a rocky way,

Against the paradox of yesterday….

I Change

Like a caterpillar with wings, as day turns night,

There's change through actions, at twilight.

Things that were not done come into existence,

On a path of enmity, there's need for self-defense.

Like a second gone null, and the wind that changes course,

Not the will of the mind, but results of a reigning force;

The heart remains the heart, and the mind remains aligned,

The person that once was can be deeply still defined….

But the present has struck, for actions to adjust,

There are things that may be done, things that are a must.

I fetch water in drought, but shelter from the rain,

The passions of the deepest heart, such passions, still remain.

Don't judge me, dear brother, let him who greens the trees,

Let him who sweets the honey from the bottom of the bees.

Pray for me, oh sister, don't leave me all alone,

In times when I have fallen, don't leave me on my own.

As blood floods our veins, so shall changes for you and I,

Shadow me from the rain; wipe my tears when I cry.

The circumstances change, so doth the sinful soul,

But all I ask and plea, protect me from the cold.

Confusing Times

These are times you think the most,

Times you sink from coast to coast...

And these are times you're high and low,

When you're not sure which way to go!

It's not too clear if you're getting worst,

When you don't know how to quench the thirst...

You hurt and heal and fill and crave,

Times of worth are real, times you kill and save…

Sometimes the rain is like the sun,

When the ounce is like the ton!

Confusing times, so worth the ache,

These are times we undertake…

Losing times, when victory is nigh,

Choosing times when you laugh and cry.

But worthy are times you maintain great might,

In twilight's plight, stay and fight!

In This Hard Time

You must be strong in this hard time,

You must keep trying and stop the crying!

Hard times are meant to be, be strong,

Walk with God as you move along!

You must be brave, bold and brave,

Forget the trails of yesterday's grave!

Mountains are a must, so thrust,

To make it through, I say you must!

You must partake of the heavenly bread,

You must indulge in the Master's stead!

Be steady oh one, oh one who is lost,

I say you can, can pay the cost!

You must be strong in these long days,

Grace your ways with the alms of praise...

Oh, one of God, be strong, be strong,

Go on and on, just move along!

Love...

Oh Woman

You're Gods greatest gift to man,
How you make him satisfied.
God's sacred little plan,
To save him from the tears he's cried.

You're the rescue he desires,
The savior that he requires.
You smile to make him right,
How you fill his heart with such delight.

You've done what none can do,
Crafted heaven to shine on you!
And you sigh to make him strong,
Fit safe in his arms where you belong.

The corridors of my heart are blocked,
On your doors oh Lord I've knocked.
Because none can fill my empty soul,
So send me her, to warm my cold.

Never Knew Love

I never knew love,

Till there was you love!

Like a day with a new love,

Is what you do to me, set me free!

Never had love, like a glad love,

Tis what I knew, sad love!

Till there was you love,

Love, I'll never eschew love!

It's alright love, let's fight love,

Plight through the night holding tight love!

Let's endeavor to endure, we're sure love,

That if we stay, in the day, we'll have more love!

Stand firm love, when it burns let us burn,

Still we're good, in the end, we will earn love!

Let's go love, row our tides still we're tight,

Every plight through the night, we'll be alright love!

Forever Valentine

It's never new, what you do to me,

You saturate the wings of time and fill my destiny!

Days are never empty, you fill me with your perfume,

You are a flower in the wind that never ceases to bloom!

Oh woman, you're God's greatest gift to mankind,

Without you we are nothing but blind leading the blind.

A perfect design, you fit the arms so well,

My words are faint, yet they can tell!

It never ends, the comfort that you've given,

You are the epitome of heaven!

Oh, gift from God, you resonate forever,

Your joy is my endeavour!

Accept us as we are,

Thou twinkle little star!

You nourish from the vine,

My forever valentine!

I Could Be the One

If I could be the one,

The one to make you smile!

Under the piercing sun,

My life would be worthwhile!

For if I could be the choice elect,

My joy would be as the towers erect!

The archeries of my heart they flow,

With memories of not too long ago!

I miss you I say out loud,

My love's strong rage can part a crowd!

How I miss you, I say with might,

Lately you're away and never in sight!

Thought I might write you this poem I rhyme,

I might sing you this melody I chime!

Let me be the one to empower your need,

Let me be the one to heal you as you bleed!

I can be the one dear soul,

For us to walk until we're old!

Two old souls, looking back, having fun,

Can I be that one? Can I be the one?

My Emblem

Each scenery stems a joy in my soul,

Every page of your charm in my spirit patrol...

And every laughter unfolds a different gem,

Your smile unwraps my heart, my Emblem!

I can't escape your presence, you revolve my intellect,

You digest in my thoughts and my space of being affect...

Oh, angel in the distance,

You conquer my resistance!

And penetrate, my love,

You ascend and descend like a dove...

It's more divine, how you empower my impression,

Then you scribe on my heavens and we become one!

Mama's Love

Mama's Love is like a storm, knocking me out,

I can't contend with mama's love; it pours all about.

It rises to the summit, and reigns with the sun,

Her love stands alone, mama's love is number one.

It cuts me deep inside, from her love I cannot hide,

And though she casts the rod, her arms are opened wide.

Oh, I'm incarcerated, overwhelmed and saturated,

Far away, I remember mama; she can't be fabricated.

Time has bred the distance; still there's no resistance,

Mama's love can swim! It quells with such insistence.

It is armored, mama's love can persuade,

I feel no pain, can't abstain; her love's my barricade.

Her love climbs the mountain; it wrestles like a lion,

Then pours like a fountain, from the hills of Zion.

Oh, I miss my mama, I long for her like there's no tomorrow,

Mama's love it aims and triggers; it bores me like an arrow.

A Whisper

When I seek a word, I often deflate,

Such words won't find their way.

Yet a whisper is a song that waits,

Can a listening ear, hear what whispers say?

OH, that a heart would unwind a whisper's cry,

That thy spirit would translate my sigh!

For yet my words are few if spoken,

My speech is lost, so hear my pen.

And though my ink is few and fade,

A little pen can persuade.

That my love for you is bold,

If a whisper's sigh should be untold.

That my whisper is heard, 'I crave,'

For it to be known, 'love's strong rage!

And my whisper's true, though fade and few,

But bold, as strong a hold, it's true, that **'I Love You!'**

To See Her Again

I love to love her, in every beat,

My heart is a trumpet, each archery a fleet.

To love her is a bottomless glass in time,

Each beat of my heart churns with her rhyme!

And her smile, it absolves my day,

With a grace so spaceless, she takes me away!

How I miss her, no pen can tell such tale,

No sigh will do, no pamper can pierce such ail!

How I long to be strong again,

For the sheet of her warm membrane…

And I cry with a silence; I survive with a pain,

For I long, how I long, to see her again!

Worthwhile

There's more to being around you,

To taste the music of your smile.

I find that when I'm around you,

My life becomes worthwhile!

And I couldn't sleep last night,

For within every second was the thought of you.

My pillow so crowded with a song I now rewrite,

Every word is true; you render me new!

When morning comes, and I don't see your face,

I begin to hunger for your embrace...

And I thank the heavens beyond the dew,

That every part of me is deeply in love with you!!

Thanks for coming, I'm lost for words to express,

I'm filled with your beauty that in my heart, undress…

And your smile, when I see you smile,

Heaven is opened, and life becomes worthwhile!!

What If

What if I say 'I Love you?

Would you radiate that bounteous smile?

If I say forgive me, I'm true,

Come with me, walk with me down the aisle….

And if I write you a poem I rhyme,

Could I serve you the music of time?

Inhale me with your love my queen,

What if I smile, would it be seen?

I ponder with the thought of your majesty,

Come with me; girl come with me…

What if you come, will you realize?

That your presence overshadows my eyes…

For sure I have the most precious one,

She sticks with me till the day is done!

I'm a man most satisfied,

She is my charm; she is my bride!

Collide

I run from your presence to somewhere I can't go,

I'm filled with pretense, the grief that I show.

But when I go left, I turn right; I can't hide,

And I finally find you and I collide.

I run to the stars when you're on the moon,

And wish it was morning when it's only noon.

In my heart that is tender is so much pride,

Baby, I conclude to find you, and I collide.

I'm wet in your love though I want to be dry,

Fate only knows for you I would die.

I collapse in the ocean on your roaming tide,

Just to know inside, you and I collide.

I want to be lost, but with you, I am found,

Though I am so conscious, in you I am drowned.

You open your arms so welcoming wide,

And I arose to find you, and I collide.

When I go left, I turn right I can't hide,

I get to know inside; you and I collide.

My Dearest!

You cross my mind like the wind cross the trees,

And sway with my thoughts like sand in the breeze.

I greed you, when in and out I breathe so dare,

I wonder if you're close, for I feel your presence near.

You dwell in my heart like cream in a cone,

And cement in my memory like minerals to a stone.

I feel you in my biome a thousand miles away,

And carry you in my soul from day onto day.

I digest you in me like words to the ears,

Your whisper resounds and rids my fears.

Just to glance your presence, I'd merge with the tide,

To travel with the oceans, to feel you close beside.

And words lose all meaning, tongues cannot utter,

Lips become frost as in loneliness, I stutter.

My heart tends to crave for you to the sight,

The stars how they glitter, as I greed in the night.

Her Ecstasy

Her coat is covered with the ecstasy she carries,

The joy of her embrace and the beauty she marries!

How I ponder on the prudence of her smile,

Rest with me, my dearest, rest with me a while!

My inner realm, she reaches this far with her grace,

When forever is done, I'll rekindle to feel her embrace.

Whisper my dear; speak to the surrounds of my soul,

Your spirit is near; it chills every piece of my whole!

As a wind, you swirl on the wings of my heart,

You're nature's best, a season of sensuous art…

That how great you are, absolve me in your ecstasy,

Oh gentle star, drown me, and don't let me be!

There's never a dull moment in time,

Not a sigh without the churn of your rhyme!

Don't save me from this ecstasy she bestows,

Let me free with the joy, tis the peace that I know!

The Love of God

It is titanically high, gigantically strong,

And it chants with a one to the last furlong….

As a tide, it rants its rage,

It wrestles every demon every age!

What a love, for it indwells every ache,

A light that is always awake!

It climbs every hill with a drill,

It performs its mission, for this is its will!

Oh, what a love, that patiently waits for all,

With an arm far stretched, awaiting our call…

In the heart's great sigh, Jah Love is by,

It pampers our tears when we cry!

What a love, that stubbornly haunts with grace,

It penetrates every wound that scars our face.

The love of God never diverts nor derail,

So wide, so high, so deep in depth, this love can never fail!

I'll Remember You

You've played with my feelings like a child in the yard,

You snap on my intellect with no mercy, so hard.

I go about the day with the memory that lives on so true,

There wasn't a sad moment to share, and I'll remember you.

I blame nature for introducing you, to impact my emotions,

I blame the past, it can't be changed, the future is no more.

I breathe every minute with a smile behind the blue,

Amidst all the sorrow and pain, I will remember you.

I still search for the light that terminates the dark,

For that gentle heart, that'll bring back the spark.

That brings out the colour in me, some one true,

Till the rain is at ending, and eagles don't soar, I'll remember you.

Will tears ever cease, loneliness decease, will stars ever
shine?

Will the deed of my heart ever come to be mine?

I know you've gone on, everything that you do I agree,

But all that I ask, could you please…. Remember me.

Abide My Love

When the light's asleep, I come to You,

When the night is young and green...

I till and toil the night right through,

To be affectioned in Thy Being!

I cry when I'm alone,

When You never pick up the phone!

Tears explode, still I'm guided along,

Weakness tarry, yet You harmonize my song!

My Christ, my sacred friend,

With a pamper He'll attend...

Oh, linger along the way,

Abide my love, till day!

Faith

Every Word

Every word of God is pure,

Every promise is sure!

The wind of His breath will ever keep us secure...

His Word is a lure,

Agape our cure!

It will cut and divide and indwell at the core!

What a comfort to know,

He'll never let go...

As a light in our tunnels, He waters our seeds as we grow!

On the tides when we flow,

He Abides as we row!

As we conquer the currents, His lead we follow!

Closer than a brother, and a mother and a friend,

Holy Spirit is there to the end!

When we walk and we talk, when we press on our way,

It is Suffice to say you are never alone,

So, find rest with the knowledge that He makes you His
own!

Don't Hide from Me

Why do You hide, Oh mighty God?

 Why should You hide from me?

I search the depths to feel you close,

Still I never get grasp of Thee!

My yearn, as sorrow hurts,

With pain that clogs and girths!

Oh Christ, Oh Christ, where have You gone?

Dear Christ, please come and on me dawn...

The desserts are wide as heavens spread,

My gentle joy, oh come instead!

Father way beyond my reach,

Teardrops are rain, Lord I beseech!

So, pour in my direction,

So, quake with Your affection...

For if I try, I ever fail,

When I try the err prevail!

I'll never cease to rise,

I press to reach the prize!

My king, why should you hide from me,

Christ my King, oh give me Thee!

Consider

Consider the trees and the whistle of the wind,

Consider the birds in the sky; they are pinned…

The sound of the waves in the abundant deep,

The cry of the brave as the sigh of a weep.

The grace of the creek, consider the sound,

Consider the rains when on roofs they pound!

Consider the quakes as they move along faults,

Hear the creation as Jah, it exalts!

Now, Consider the man who is stuck on his way,

And behold the light that brightens his day...

Consider the cold, the cold of the hurt,

Ponder the cries, and the craves of the earth!

Yet consider the hill from whence cometh our strength,

the love from its rays in its width and its length!

Consider the sunshine, as it basks the naked skins,

and the moments of joy on the earth when it spins.

Consider the all and see the king,

The Light of Life in everything!

How great the hands that made all these?

Consider the grace that sets us at ease!

You're Presence

Your Presence permits me a praise,

It lasts and lingers for days...

How Your Presence penetrate perpetually,

Your Presence sets me free; You set me free!

And I fall as I bawl in Your Presence,

I call till I hear, For Your Presence is near!

Your Presence, it fills my gap, my heart it claps,

As I leap for Joy, it raptures me; it Raps!!

When I'm far away, Your Presence surrounds,

Such melody when Your Presence pounds!

How You haunt me with goodness and grace,

Oh, if I run You come, if I erase You trace!

What Love, it rains on pains and chains,

It rescues me; it sets me free; it fills my veins!!

If I mourn You Adorn, with a precious pamper,

And camp in me, like musical amps in me!

In His Presence, in the Presence of the Lord,

We ride in one accord, till we concord!

How His Presence penetrate perpetually,

He sets me free, yes, His Presence sets me free!

With Love, My Valentine

How do I put pen to page?

To tell this truth that cannot age…

I look within my rest, and wrestle with the vine,

And present, to you, with love, my Valentine!

I find courage though I'm broken,

To unwrap to you my token…

Lost a wretched, I stand in the midst of dying,

And I run to you, with love, my Valentine.

How simple is a heart's humble crave?

Oh, I long to be Your slave.

I'm lost in Your benignity, drunken in the wine,

So, I perish, to live, with love, my Valentine.

Take me as is, without any form of comeliness,

But though the least, I fight for your arrest….

Alight in me and let me be, capture my design,

Christ, my Lord, am as I am; with love, my Valentine!

We Climb

On the hills of God, we climb,

As we crawl through the crevices of time.

As a light with ray, we reach with faith,

Just to sup upon our Master's Plate!

On the Holy mountain of Jah, we stride,

In the midst of the middle, He'll ever abide!

With a confidence, we challenge the way,

Just to sit in His presence and pray!

Oh, Holy Hill, where truth is found,

The grace and music of His sound.

As birds, we churn, "glory to the Lamb,"

Because He is, I am, I am!

Sup upon the Lamb, feast upon the bread,

Consider how He died, consider how He bled!

Yet for us, His wounds were calculated,

For then, we could be fully emancipated.

And on, and on, we climb,

To sing to Him, our rhyme.

He is the light as we reach in faith,

We shall feast upon our Master's plate!

I Do

What I desire not to do, I do,

I fight my fleshy treasures, yet they defeat me too.

I armour and parade, I girth my stance,

I fall from grace and die at once.

I plead my cause; I can't comply,

Oh, who will save me when I cry?

My vanity knocks me over, lost in the wild,

Fractured and bruised and obedient as a child.

I climb on His Holy Mountain,

For I know, there is a fountain.

Filled with a Lambs Great Sacrifice,

For "who can save me but the Christ?"

My sins have me in captivity,

Oh, I'm challenged by my livity.

Comely Jah, Thy priesthood conquers all,

You project to my sound, "hear me as I bawl!"

Mercy Seat

I run to the Mercy Seat,

Hoping He will quench my thirst.

I marvel with a bellow at his feet,

Jah tends me when me teardrops burst!

I travail with a song all night long,

I partake with the weak; I'm not strong.

But my Christ is a tower for me,

He rushes like the wind to set me free.

I rejoice with the angels on high,

For He heard me when I poured my cry!

And I run to the Mercy Seat,

I marvel with a bellow at His feet.

Again

When morning surrenders, I'm there again,
Calling and bawling, I pour my pain!
Before the sun, I rise and complain,
Cries in my eyes, gall in my vein!

But I abide where strings play a song,
I tarry in labour as I'm moving along.
I'm not strong, yet till mercy responds,
I appeal to a virtue that bonds.

My tears are as flood at heaven's door,
Till it rains, won't mercy drill my shore?
I wait the more, committed in praise,
Touched to the core, I lament for my days!

Still, hope abides and alights and awakes,
He pampers wounds and comforts aches.
Yet I bawl, when I pain,
And I'm at His mercy seat again!

Come By

I'm heavy with a burden, You see!

Hear these groans that groan in me.

The depression of my soul is nigh,

Come by, my Christ, come by.

Remind me oh God, of a Potter to clay,

Walk with me when it's dark at day.

Hear my bellows blow, strings of praise,

My heart is weary but dead you raise!

If a son should pour gall at Your feet,

You are sure to make an agony sweet…

My tears they unite at heaven's door,

For sure, my God will save, for sure!

So, meet me at my deepest tear,

Come near my Christ, come near.

And if I forget, remind me again,

Still, if I forget, remind me, Lord, again!

Great Father

Great Father over all,

Hear my cry, Oh, Lord!

It's my stance, lest I fall,

I shall abide till we concord!

Abba, how mighty Your reign,

Tender Thy love that breaks every chain.

Oh, reach at the stool of Your throne,

For I bellow in the deep all alone…

Still, I know You are ever-present,

Tending daily to my cares.

Your mercy clothes the peasant,

When we bawl You bottle tears!!

My agony never stops,

I'm empty till you fill my cup…

Oh Father, great over all,

Hold my hands, lest I fall!!

The Joy

The Joy of the Lord is my strength,

It alights my proceedings; I cannot prevent.

I'm captured by the rapture, lost on a high,

For in my space's just God and I.

This benignity of grace, I cannot unfold,

I inflate in the splendor, and Jah, I behold.

Warming my soul, affecting my wound,

In His arms I'm embellished, in Christ, I'm ballooned!

He stretches my smile with no bounds,

Oh, what a Joy that fills my surrounds.

That even my tears are crowned with stance,

I'm engulfed in the music of a heavenly romance.

Nothing else can take Your place,

You conquer deep, and all erase.

Oh, my Lord, my strength has been Thy Joy,

The yoke is easy, the enemy within You destroy!!

I'm Free

The thing my soul so loved,

Is the thing that I abhor.

To a thing, my soul was gloved,

A thing I do not want no more!

To a thing was I once slave,

Is the thing that used to be.

But Christ came in my grave,

And with His Love, had set me free!!

Now, this thing my soul revolts,

I'm strapped onto His divine bolts...

Who the Son sets free, He liberates,

My soul is far from what it hates….

And the thing I loved, I now despise,

A Light has come and made me wise.

And the thing that held to me,

Is the thing from which **'I'm Free!'**

Delve, My Christ!

Lift me to Your realm,

Force beyond my introspect.

Grandeur with the helm,

My space of being affect!

Adapt me to Your reign,

Oh, Majesty Who girths with strength.

From Thy lofty throne arraign,

I give You my consent.

Conquer my vanity,

Connect broken dreams.

Transcend me to sanity,

Almighty Might redeem!!

Dwell in an earthen vessel,

Make my heart Your home.

Save me from this wrestle,

Come park in my biome!

Cradle at my crave,

Till faith will find its stance...

Bring to quiescence, the enemy's rage,

Delve my Christ delve my expanse!!

In a Moment

The gentleness of the moment,

Rushing across my mind...

A calm and gentle savor,

In a moment, I unwind...

I delve the eternal realm,

As the moment passes by.

Quieted by the peace,

I clasp my hands as the heavens cry!

I'm transcended to the spirit,

Where perfection is my tale...

In a moment, I dine the Divine,

His love sets me a sail!

Raptured by its glory,

I cross the great divine...

Immortality and the mortal meets,

Where Majesty and I collide...

Oh, splendor of the moment,

You lift me beyond my mind.

Oh, lofty realm of Christ,

In a moment I unwind!!

Still I Stand

Still, I stand, anchored by His Spirit,

Pressed on every side, yet I will never quit.

Christ is my resurrection; death is gone away,

Christ is my perfection, I sit, and I pray.

I hold, constrained by His hands,

Tamed by His love, I adapt to His plans.

'Woe is me, 'I am utterly undone,

So, I rest, rooted deeply, I rest in His Son…

He chastens me; He renders His rebuke,

I can't unwind such paradox; He feeds me in the brook…

He leads me to perfection; OH, I bawl,

He keeps me in the deep; I'm led by His holy haul…

I thank my God, I hope in His grace,

Tilled in my soil, for sure, for sure, I'll see His face!

I cry at my Saviour, 'how long, my Christ, how long?'

Lord, I've been weak, but forever You are strong!

I Weep

I weep, till depths are found,

I roar, I must rebound…

I must adorn myself with a song,

I'm strong, with Jah, I'm strong!

I bawl, the bellow blows,

I rise, for Christ, He rose…

My deepness is as an eternal want,

But "hear me, Thou near me," I chant!

Conquer these fears that haunt in me,

Have mercy, my God, set me free!

Harken my plea, Christ unfailing…

Touch my wounded wailing!

For the pressure pains in stings,

My God, You know all things…

As the waters flow, my cry is nigh,

Fill this temple, Christ come by!

My weep is as a mighty river,

Oh Jah, my God, you must deliver!

They pest me when my tears do flow,

Christ, you know, my Christ, you know!

Rescue me, oh rescue me from my captivity,

For Him who you set free, my God is free!

Look and Behold

The seas, the breeze, the trees,

And the cattle on the hill...

The earth is the Lord's, all knees,

The peace, the man, the will!

Take a look, the eyes and the view,

All of creation testifies anew…

That the Lord has fashioned the glory,

That the Lord has scribed the story!

The sounds of the quiescence,

Of all that come from whence…

Are the Lord's, as He permits,

The awe in every splendor He knits!

The times and seasons as spices,

The reason for things, devisor, and devices!

For Christ is first and last,

The future, the present, the past…

Cease and ponder, of the lightning and thunder,

What Jah has united, who shall put asunder?

For He breathes into the expanse,

And all He commands come at once!

How mighty, the Almighty, His ways,

We surrender every praise…

The days, the time, the view,

Jah created all, and you!

Mercy Me

Mercy me, oh Him that He hears,

Mercy, my sorrows, oh mercy, my tears.

Pamper my weary, my loss of Thy grace,

Replenish my broken, rest at my base.

Mercy me, oh Him that He heals,

Pardon my wrongs, every pain that I feel.

Sap on my raindrops, as a shelter and rest,

Mercy me please, as this day I confess.

I'm thirsty for you, so lost down the gully,

How wrong that I am, I question my folly.

But mercy my tears, that bleed like a river,

Oh, mercy me, Savior, as birth just deliver.

Can agony get deeper? my aches endure,

Find me, I plea; I'm lost I implore.

Mercy my crave, oh Him who He hears,

Mercy my worry, oh condone on my tears.

I Miss You

In pouring rain, there's so much pain, pain to return,

On weakened knees, help me, please, take me in concern.

I drift away, but feel so lost, lost without Your touch,

I'm lonely here; I feel the frost, I miss you Lord so much.

Yours love heals, Your Spirit saves; grace that pardons sin,

With every breath, I shout out loud; I give my everything.

I humbly plea, I gently beg, I come to you as such,

My veins are sealed, I must be healed, I miss You very much.

The love that shines in the dark, the feet that calms the sea,

Without Your presence, where'd I go? I just couldn't be me.

My heart it bleeds, it cries a yonder, it seeks a hiding place,

I'm gone away; collapsed in grief, Lord, I need your grace.

I've fallen deep, from Your throne, I am so all alone,

Like a single crow that soars the sky, Lord I'm on my own.

As a river runs and never dries, I cry without your touch,

There's never hope without You near, I miss You Lord so much.

Lust

How precious are her promises?

She spills a coloured ray.

How prudent is a sacred smile?

That tells a tale from far away.

What grace that holds me captive,

That nullifies the crave.

And refracts to haunt the distant eyes,

Till I come to be a slave.

The sight cannot be gratified,

For light was never there.

Her platter serves me lies,

Darkness spawns and comes her heir.

Oh, save me from her resonance,

That knocks an opened door.

She brings a case of fraudulence,

Yet keeps haunting me the more.

Beware oh man of many faiths,

For there awaits but only one.

Her colours assure a certain death,

Life is in the Christ; the way is in the Son!!

Rectify My Pain

Rekindle oh fire of mine, oh warmth with a beam,

Report to me, oh lost, come to the land where I dream.

The moments are bitter, as I trod a path of stain,

Just forward from whence you came, rectify my pain!

The leaves have dried; the birds drop their wings,

Heaven closes its windows and all, but mercy brings.

Oh, Being who washes torment, abide upon my strain,

Pardon the wrongs of yesterday, rectify my pain.

I harness what I sow; I earn the labour of my years,

Oh rescue, dear Keeper, confiscate these fears.

I rebuke the folly of my walk, the vain of my run,

Like a breath gone astray, I wander beneath the sun.

But low, I ask for anchor, to save me as I go,

I know Your worth oh Giver, help me here below.

My words are dear; Oh, send me rain,

Abound upon my bitter strain and rectify my pain!

How Great

How great is our God in all the earth?

How great is his Majesty?

He sends the sun to sooth the hurt,

And the northern winds to pamper me!

How great the King Who made all things?

Mighty Is His Kingdom's reign!

Of a melody of joy my soul it sings,

For He sends His Word to rid my pain!

How great His name, I sing a song?

My heart is elated, my soul it Hums...

He walks with me as I move along,

His will be done, His Kingdom come!

I must pronounce that God is great,

I must invite before its late!

Come sup the sup, come taste the savory,

Come feel these winds that pamper me!

About the Author

Orlando Rowe is an author and also the founder of the motivational website poweredtoempower.com. He holds a Master's Degree in Theology and a Bachelor of Science Degree. Orlando's passion is to see people living their best lives, and as a result, he helps individuals in achieving this. He currently works as a counsellor in the Canadian Youth Justice department.

Visit the Powered to Empower at www.poweredtoempower.com to view some of his other work.

Other Book: **Broken: When the pieces fall apart.**